WHY I

A YOUNG BLACK MAN

VOTED FOR TRUMP

2016 FROM THE EYES OF GENERATION Z

Nicaleb Gedeon

1

THE INTRODUCTION

Starting a conversation like this is not easy, so instead of trying to find some sequence of words that will lead in, I opted to admit how difficult it is, and jump into this. Given the title of this book, there are a few reasons why you probably decided to pick it up. You are a Republican who is curious as to what got me to vote for the party that has been labeled racist wrongfully, you are a black Democrat who wants to see how I could make such a foolish discussion "against my self interest," or you're a snowflake who is prepared to attack me because I dare have an opinion that doesn't match your identity politics and isn't the same opinion as yours. Whatever reason you decided to pick up this book, I plan on making it worthwhile, and maybe even drop a few little-known facts along the way. And for the snowflakes who are going to read this, I appreciate you actually looking at a different point of view that doesn't line up with your own: this is by the way how civilized people engage with one another. Enough about you, I'll get to my story.

2

MY POLITICAL JOURNEY

This journey is a long and convoluted one, but one that was necessary for me reaching the "radical" decision I've made. It all started after Obama became president, at this time, I was a 5th grader, and our whole class had to watch the inauguration since it was a historic time in our American history, and rightfully so, I was of course more pumped about not having to do anything all day. At the time, I knew little about politics, as was expected of a kid in elementary school, so I was hyped like every other kid in class both black and white. "First black president whoop whoop," I said. After this monumental event, the hype lasted a couple of days, since the other kids were still talking about it, but as more interesting things happened in our adolescent lives, this monumental event quickly faded into the back of my mind. There would be occasional events involving our black president that even the kids would talk about, but it was nothing important to me. After the initial hype, things went back to normal, we had a president doing presidential things, and I was a young boy doing young boy things, life went on. Years went by, and I paid very little attention to politics. I had: girls, school, church, sports, parents, and my squad to worry about.

Life was chill, went through a few crushes, friends came and went, and I was slowly growing into the man I am today. Then, of course, the re-election came, and it was almost just like I was a kid again, but something was different, I had a slight feeling towards our president that made me want him to get knocked off his throne of black votes. If you ask me where these feelings came from, I would have no answer for you. You would hear me on the bus saying "Obama sucked," and asking others "what good did he actually do, besides being the first black president?" This wasn't taken well by my black friends, I would say "there is no way he gets re-elected, he did nothing," they would respond with nothing countering my statement, but sticking to the script about him being a black president, one even responded with, "my president is black, and my Lambo is blue." As you all well know, the next school day, I had to return with my head hanging low. I was wrong, and of course, I had to hear about it, and thankfully, it didn't last too long, no one cared about politics at the time, and neither did I.

Throughout all of these years and through all these events, I was being molded into something that most black kids are, but don't seem to label it as such….. a conservative, yes the dreaded conservative. I was raised in church, though a misguided denomination, I was taught the essential elements that made up a biblical Christian: love thy neighbor, do not steal, don't be greedy, save yourself for God's right choice for you, homosexuality is a sin, men and women have different roles and abilities, etc. I had good values instilled in me, and I tried to live by them as best as I could. All this, of course, translated to a very conservative individual, though I didn't know it till the 2016 presidential election which genuinely put me in a position to truly seek and discover what party and candidate best identified with who I was.

Throughout the beginning of the election, I wasn't paying attention to much politics; I had the most beautiful girl in the world I was trying to convince to date me and college to worry about. I was just honestly relieved that Obama wasn't the president anymore Change was promised and change never came. The fact that Obama was a Democrat is probably what got me to do what most black Americans have been conditioned not to do, actually look at both sides and make your own decision. That being said, I am a college-aged individual, so of course, I started looking for some videos on YouTube. My feed became more and more littered with political videos, and one day, I stumbled into a Ben Shapiro thug life video and was instantly hooked; the way he demolished the liberal lies with such ease, accompanied by facts, and statistics was a straight-up masterpiece. This leads me to look through almost all of his videos, from debates to speeches at college campuses. He did something that I have come to see never happens with people on the left and shows true skill; he would have a question and answer portions at the end of his speeches and tell those who disagreed with him to be sent to the front of the line. It was a well-established fact that they would be met with respect, but also be utterly obliterated by sourced facts and a well-articulated response. I have yet to see someone leave the mic without having their question thoroughly answered. Although this is the story about how I came to vote for Trump, I'm sure your starting to think this is a promotional for Ben, so that will be enough about that political genius for this time. Along with Ben, some others got the conversation going in my mind, like Crowder(who is tied for first place with Ben), Dinesh D'Souza, Milo, and a few others.

What these people did for me is pivotal to the person I am today. They exposed what I was told I should think to be completely false. I was told that blacks were still at a disadvantage in America because of white people and "institutional racism." I was told that women were being paid less than men for the same work because they were born with the wrong set of chromosomes. I was told that if you are a Christian and a gay couple asks you to bake them a cake for their wedding, and you say no because you will not support what is against God, you should lose your business and source of income for your family. I was told that your pursuit of life, liberty, and happiness given by God could be stripped from you if your mother believes you are a burden upon her life or a mistake. I was told that if you came here illegally, you are entitled to the social welfare that I pay into, and jobs that are for the citizens of this great United States and those who followed our rules to get here. I was told that Islam is a religion of peace, when everywhere mass immigration of people who subscribe to this religion occurs rape skyrockets, violent crimes increase, and terror attacks become just another occasion. And most important of all, I was told that if I don't believe these things I'm a racist, sexist, bigot, and homophobe. As I became more aware of what I already valued, as well as what I came to value the more I knew, I realized the Republican party was the place for me. Little did I know, that I was about to embark on a journey I was not at all ready for.

When the primaries were over, and we knew who would be running for both parties, I knew this wasn't going to be a walk in the park. On one side, there was a woman who was going to run on the platform her predecessor used. Chanting it was time for the first woman to be president much like Obama capitalized on his complexion to gain the upper hand; a woman who was caught violating protocol, at the magnitude that would put anyone without her last name in jail, as well as, causing the deaths of some of our finest. On the other hand, we had a man who by no means would not have been my first pick;

he was a businessman who wasn't afraid to say what he wanted since he was not a politician with people in his pockets. He actually spoke about the people who would come to vote him, not just appealing to one sex and calling the other racist. It was absolutely an easy choice for me, but the hard part was the fact that I was a black man. I don't think to this day I've met more than one black person excluding myself that voted for Trump. I had stepped off the reservation, although I was never attacked, I had a sense of being excluded even more than I already was from the black community. I wasn't too foreign to this feeling, I listen to different music, I treat people differently, and I valued different things compared to the mainstream depiction of the black American. Anyways, after the options were laid out, I went full blown Trump mode, that crooked chick needed to be defeated if we were going to keep America alive and flourishing. I know that sounds drastic, but I will explain further on how I was right to feel that way.

I spoke out about how I was rooting for Trump and people were taken by surprise. I would emphasize it when talking semi-politically with someone, especially my white friends or white strangers. I did this because the media had painted Trump and everyone who voted for him a racist, so people who supported him were afraid to talk about it for fear that I was one of those other people. The relief that washed over them was always a delight and they would begin to talk about their opinions with no fear, with someone who they were originally too terrified to do so with.

The opposite, as you can guess was true when I told a black person, they would look at me like I was a buffoon. At this point, I wouldn't even bother trying to explain my reasons, because I knew it was force-fed to them to think Trump was a racist, and I was either a blind kid or a traitor to the black race. So me talking to someone about politics was almost exclusively with white people, and I wasn't happy with that. I wanted to talk to all people with the same ability and capacity. The political climate has been charged to the point that it was almost impossible for anyone to talk to anyone with differing opinions. You can try all you want to disagree, but this was because of the race-baiting tactics of the left. And to clarify, I do not hate everyone on the left; I just don't like what it has caused.

So, if you are still reading this and feel like I am attacking you personally, I apologize, I am trying to tell my story the best I can. I appreciate you still reading.

As the election proceeded, race relations plummeted, Black Lives Matter became ridiculously violent, feminist began attacking all straight white males, fake hate crimes were repeatedly reported to make the right look racist and bigoted. The closer it got to the end, the more dangerous it was, videos of a poor old white man being dragged out of his car and beaten in the street for simply having some indication that he supported our president, videos of swarms of blacks marching, and calling for pigs in a blanket. It was a large step back in our progression towards a society that is united. I was one of those black people that denounced Black Lives Matter, because unlike the others; I know that this separation of people in our country would lead to its downfall. I also seemed to be one of a few blacks who realized that the violence was counterproductive to anything rooted on peace, it showed blacks in a violent light, showed that we are irrational, it showed that the statistics about how much crime we commit is becoming truer than ever, it showed that we are incapable of discussing our problems without aggression. And I know all black people are not like this, and I know we as a people are capable of great things when we truly put in our best effort like all great people. I made sure to show my hate for this movement on my Facebook. I know, I know, I know what the heck is that going to do, and who uses Facebook anymore. But hear me out, I managed to spark up a lot of discussions, which in my opinion is better than sitting around letting everyone think all black people were like this. I had to show that #NotAllBlackPeople were like or supported this idiotic activity. I'll be sure to return to this group later to bring facts to shut this group down later on.

Finally, it was drawing to the last days before the election: I was just tad bit nervous, but ohhh sooo ready for this. All positions aside for a minute, this is my first time getting to vote, and I feel like one shouldn't complain about the president if they didn't make an effort to go out and place their ballot.

My Facebook was littered with my position, hoping that people would get psyched about this election as much as I was. I was even more hyped when my Democrat parents and little sisters joked around and said, raise your hand if you think Trump isn't going to be president and they all raised their hands. Then my father, who mind you has all the values of a Republican and doesn't believe in not one of the positions of the democrat party, said to me, "He is not going to win, look at the show of hands in the house that he will lose," as if to say that this show of hands illustrated that it was impossible for him to win. A few things can make a man more determined for something to happen then when his whole family is betting that he is wrong.

Election day finally rolls up, and it is game time. I am less active on my social media; all the liberal polls are saying there isn't a chance that my man Trump is going to win, all the mainstream media is laughing up a storm, thinking that Hillary had this "fool" beat. The best thing I saw throughout all this was MSNBC showing a map of the country and trying to map for Trump what would have to happen for him to actually win, the states that he would have to turn red to win, and the states he would have to hold. They were just laying on the paint; Trump is doomed!!!! Then the election finally starts that afternoon. I am so focused on this, and I don't know what to do, so I watch a bunch of YouTube videos while checking up on it. It starts off really slow, and when states are finally starting to show where they are leaning, I start getting nervous. They are somewhat neck and neck; then Trump would seem to have the upper hand and then Hillary. While this is happening I am watching some news stations and one of the mainstream news networks who had started off showing the probability of Trump winning close to two percent, starts to increase it. First, they aren't too worried; then as the results start rolling out, Trump inches towards the fifty percent probability mark, their faces start to lose that winning glow. When he breaks the fifty percent and just kept climbing, I could feel the low come across my face. Unfortunately, I had work in the morning, and I wasn't going to lose too much sleep for this. So I went to sleep with trump pulling ahead, when I woke up the next morning, I grabbed my phone to see what had become of our country, I was so happy my man Trump had prevailed against all odds. Sadly, I had to go to work so I couldn't watch the highlights till got home. When I did get home the memes and compilations were rampant, my favorite to this day is the one with every talk-show host, news anchor, and liberal celebrity that said he would never be president, then showed the States lighting up red, then them announcing that Donald J Trump will be the next president of the United States of America. Oh, it was bittersweet to see those who labeled, lied, covered, alienated, and tried to defame their opponents have to watch their opponents win, especially when they said it would never ever happen. I didn't hear about Trump winning in my house till the day after he won. My father approached me asking how happy I was that my candidate had won.... Let's just say I got a good bragging session in.

3

TRUE BLACK HISTORY

In the previous chapter, I gave you the brief overview about how I came to vote for Trump; now I will dissect why it was the best option for our country and me, especially as a black man. This is where the facts start flowing; hopefully, facts do not offend you, because as a wise man once said, "facts don't care about your feelings." Now let's begin.

Since I had to emphasize that I was a young black man that voted for Trump to get most of you to pick up this book, I will start with dropping facts on why that is. Let's start off with a history lesson, it is a well-known fact that at the beginning of our country, slavery was a problem, and it has seemed to become mainstream to say that our country was built on the back of black slaves. It actually was built on the back of indentured servants and slaves, in our history classes today of painting being bound to a master in America's past as a solely black person issue. It wasn't until 1661 that slavery was even acknowledged in any laws, Virginia was the first to do this, passing laws that made the children of slaves and their masters go by their mothers' conditions aka being a slave. This was made so that regardless of who your father was, which meant more to the future well being of a child that his mother, a slave kid would remain a slave. This was occurring around the same time that slavery was becoming something exclusively for blacks, understand I am not negating the pain and suffering African Americans endured, I am simply stating it wasn't just blacks that have been treated unfairly in the early stages of our country.

Slavery went on way too long in our country, and the blame is put exclusively on whites, but I'm sure those who are demanding whites pay reparations don't want you to know that there were a good few free black slave owners. Yes, the majority of the freed slaves that owned slaves probably did it to protect their family and close ones, but many of them also exploited this awful system to make money just like the white man. Why is it that reparations are only demanded of those who have a low level of melanin in their skin? Only 8% of white families owned slaves, and some blacks are demanding all whites pay for the sins of a few that have been dead for years? If you ask me, blaming people for your problems and asking them to give you things simply because of their race is what's the word...

RACIST. This is a crucial aspect of our history that shows this nonsense about all whites having to bear the burden of slavery as utterly ridiculous, and those who believe it to be utterly misguided or just saying whatever will get them the undeserved fruits of others hard work. If you believe there should be reparations for blacks because of slavery, don't forget you'd have to get blacks to give as well, since they participated.

Now, what we have touched on some of the slavery aspects that the left uses to try to paint white people, specifically those who don't subscribe to their narrative, it's time to touch on the histories of the Republican party. Especially to show how it has been the Republican party that is and always been on the side of the African Americans. The Republican party started around 1854 by northerners who didn't want to see slavery past 36° 30' parallel, the line that divided the pro and anti-slavery states. In the earlier moments of this party, they were called Whigs, free democrats, and other things, but in

1854, Horace Greeley coined the name Republican for the infant party. By 1855, in an unprecedented fashion,   this new kid on the block had managed to control a majority in the House of Representatives. Much like groups like Antifa and the BLM movement, when the Republican aka anti-slavery movement started to take hold, they sunk to using violence to intimidate to try and get their way. To save some time, we will fast forward a bit to the point of history that is more well known, we will talk about African Americans best friend Abraham Lincoln.

Abraham Lincoln was born in Kentucky and later moved and was raised in Indiana, as a young man he had very formal education, but was absorbed in his reading. A friend of the future president later described him as having mad intellect. Sparing all the nitty-gritty, after briefly being a captain in the Black Hawk War of 1832, Lincoln went on to study law and campaigned to obtain a seat on the Illinois State Legislature, he lost the first time around, but was later victorious in 1834. A critical aspect of this is that he ran as a Whig, which was one of the many names that were used to classify what we now call the Republican Party. After one term in Congress, he joined the New

Republican party. Heated debates with a Stephen A. Douglas over slavery in the United States transformed Lincoln into a prominent figure in national politics. In 1860, he was elected President of The United States without support from a single southern state; this enraged the south, because of his outspoken stance on slavery. Although his election wasn't the only cause of the Civil War, it was definitely a significant factor. Following the events that occurred at Fort Sumter, the war had officially begun. It wasn't until January 1, 1863, that he issued the Emancipation Proclamation, freeing all the slaves in the southern states. The war was still pushing through when it was time for Lincoln's reelection, and if it wasn't to the military victories of Ulysses S. Grant, it was a genuine possibility that he wouldn't have won. With his inauguration speech he showed that he intended to rebuild the torn country and intended not to treat the south in a sour manor. The war ended within a month. John Wilkes Booth later assassinated Lincoln, and along with his death some believed that the possibility of peacefully rebuilding without bitterness had gone with him.

At this point, you are probably wondering why I decided to go through Lincoln's life briefly. I did so to show that the Republican party was the party that was formed to bring an end to slavery, as well as, show that the man credited with freeing the slaves was one of the most prominent Republicans in history. This points out another case as to why I voted for Trump; he ran on the Republican ticket, the party that fought to give me the ability and right to vote. It is important to point out that I am not a Republican per se, I am a conservative, and that party has and is the party that mostly supports the ideals that come with being one.

After winning the Civil War, the Republicans of the north began the, seemingly just as difficult, task of helping these now freed slaves to catch up to their white counterparts in the everyday aspects of life. Educated blacks and whites came down from the north to support the newly freed blacks obtain the most important tool that could help them raise from the position they were in: an education. Blacks of all ages were gathering in schoolhouses to grab this ticket to a better life. As for those who were already educated, some had some big tasks ahead of them, particularly in the area of politics. The south under Andrew Johnson's presidency had put many barriers to keep blacks out of politics, like black codes used to regulate the lives of freed slaves. But blacks fought, organizing Black Rights Leagues throughout the south. This led to blacks flowing into politics some even going as high as the Senate.

The reconstruction also gave rise to the 14th and 15th amendments making blacks officially citizens and also stating that their rights were meant to be protected, as citizens, regardless of their race. The Reconstruction was a great movement to help those who have been enslaved, and to piece back together a torn nation, but out of this also came a counter movement. The KKK was born as a result of the moves to raise blacks to the same level as whites, as well as, how successful it was going. The KKK was an "unofficial" militant branch of the democratic party, able to go as far as threatening, beating, and killing blacks who dared to step too far out line. The Klan and some other white supremacist were responsible for taking the lives of at least 35 black officials. The Reconstruction was an essential part of black history and as a result American history.

I have been practically going through black history for the better part of this book now and you are either irritated that I am not just talking about Trump and the election or are you kinda interested in this ultra-brief rundown of black history. I am doing this to make sure we are on the same page when it comes to the events that have happened in this Great country's history. It has come to my attention that our generation doesn't seem to know these basic historical facts. I myself was not aware of some of these facts before doing some digging. Some people believe that it is the Democrats who have had the blacks backs from the start of history and that is factually incorrect. I am going over as many parts that I know some people get wrong now, so that when I get to the more accepted inaccuracies, you will see how the perception of history has been altered to fit a political agenda. And these are all a big reason why I voted for Trump, so please hang with me.

The time after the Reconstruction was a complicated time for blacks and it was by no means a great time for most. Not too long after trouble stirred and blacks had a new form of established mistreatment to overcome. In 1896 with the well-known case, Plessy vs. Ferguson, the official launch of segregation had commenced. Blacks and whites were to be treated equally, but separately from one another. There would be designated white only areas and colored areas for those with a bit more pigment in their sin. Usually, there isn't much talk about what was happening after this started, it usually skips to the events that would bring an end to it. We know about the KKK and the horrible mistreatment of blacks who were in the wrong place at the wrong time, as well as how many were treated in the court of law, but I will not delve into those because there isn't much dispute about the events that unfolded during these occurrences in history today.

Now, let's get to the biggest aspect of black history, concerning politics, that is both important and surrounded by falsehoods and political manipulation of history. What I speak of is the big switch we hear of whenever we converse and debate with today's Democrats and liberals. Before I begin deconstructing this widely believed myth, I must first explain what it states for those who have not been exposed to it. The big switch states that at some point around the beginning of the civil rights movement, there was a switch between the Democratic and Republican parties; racist and those who didn't want blacks to succeed who were in the Democratic Party moved to the Republican Party. The myth also states that it is because of this that blacks started voting overwhelmingly Democratic after voting overwhelmingly for the Republicans for ages. Now, let us examine the facts to see if this is even remotely true. For the sake of making sure this is easy to follow and that I will not be taken out of context for any reason, I will list all the facts upfront and then elaborate.

Fact #1, if any racist Democrats switched over to the Republican Party, it was undoubtedly minuet and nothing like the left are claiming happened. After looking long and hard for a list that would show such an exodus, none was to be found. One would think that such a claim would be substantiated by historical proof, wouldn't be hard to compile a list of such a movement if it did indeed happen. The most I have been able to find is about two Dixiecrats(outspoken racist members of the Democrat party) moving to the other side, and I'm going to go out on a limb here and say that isn't enough to warrant the left saying there was a big switch. It is important to make sure you clarify magnify the claim in order to come to the truth, they claim that the RACIST in the Democratic party switched sides. So you must show that the individuals are racist or hold racist views and show them switching to the other party. I encourage everyone, regardless of your political beliefs to look at this for yourself. If you can prove this fact wrong, and you can dismantle the rest of my argument, and please contact me with this finding, I'd hate to be preaching lies… cough cough.

Fact #2, blacks did not start voting overwhelmingly for Democrats because the switch had caused the other side to now have the blacks best interest in mind. Man, that's a pretty powerful statement you made there, Mr. Author, do you have any facts to back up such a claim? Indeed I do. Blacks actually started voting overwhelmingly democratic in 1932. That's almost 30 years before the civil rights moment that the left claim is what caused blacks to switch their long time friends the Republicans. Wait, Mr. Author, if it wasn't because of the changing of racism between the parties why did the blacks start voting for

Democrats in such vast numbers? It is because of the New Deal policies that President Roosevelt, as a result of the great depression, put into effect. These policies were to help those who were strongly affected by the Great Depression, among those, were ethnic minorities. Blacks decided the economic assistance proposed by Roosevelt and the Democrats was more important to them than sticking with the party that had been on their side from the very beginning. I can't blame them; they wanted to make sure they could put food on the table for their family, especially after the worst depression they had ever seen. The Democratic party continued to use the promise of economic assistance to keep the blacks in their corner, and some could easily argue that they continue to cater to blacks in such a fashion to keep them voting for them to this day, but I'm not going there for now. If you can find proof that this fact is incorrect please feel free to contact me with your findings.

Fact #3 it is not because of the Democrats that the Civil Rights Act of 1964 was passed. It was because of Republicans who pushed through the filibuster, that the Democrats had implemented, that the Civil Rights Act of

1964 was able to come to fruition. In order to overcome this historical proof that it was the republicans again that were in the blacks corner, even in a time when they have tried to teach others the contrary by attempting to use factors such as geography, with respect to the civil war, to show that it democrats were the ones that had black's best interest in mind. It is important to point out that yes, after Republicans got past the Democrat filibuster, with the help of some Democrats, the bill got passed in the house and senate. The most convincing argument that democrats try to use that help back their false claim that it was them that were truly fighting for the blacks is the fact that it was a democratic president that had signed it into law, and history can't refute that. But let's be honest, if the only reason the bill gets to the president is because of the republicans victory against the democrat filibuster and you are a democratic president and strike it down, the very crucial vote of the blacks would indefinitely return to the Republican party, demolishing any chance of Democrats winning office for many years afterward. Keep in mind that this is the same president who has been quoted saying,

"I'll have those niggers voting Democratic for 200 years." I will leave it at that, and you make with that what you will.

With the overwhelming evidence that the political parties switching did not actually happen, I continue to support the party that has had blacks back from day one, which definitely played a factor to me voting for Trump. I wish more blacks would read up on their history, so that they do not continue to disregard the other side of the political discussion completely. Thinking that everyone on the other side is a racist will blind us from potentially picking better people to represent what we truly believe and value in our country.

Now that I have cleared up some misconceptions and shown that if the historical facts aren't misrepresented, me voting for Trump actually isn't that outlandish of an idea. I have probably lingered too long in black history at this point; I will now look at the other equally important factors that lead to me voting the way I did.

4

FACTS

While the mainstream media was focusing on the heavily misrepresented, racial aspects of politics, I was busy educating myself. I was learning to become something we see less and less of: an educated voter. I was looking at things like immigration, healthcare, foreign relations, taxes, among other things. While I was trying to absorb all this important information, other crazy topics started dominating the airwaves. My boys Ben and Crowder were the first conservatives that I saw tackling these head on with no regard for the PC overlords, and it made me scratch my head.

Topics like systemic racism is still alive and well, women are being paid 77 cents on the dollar for the same work as men, free speech should be restricted, men can become women and vice versa, etc.

Before I can even touch the more serious stuff, I feel I have to get the currently hyped and easily refutable ideas out of the way. A disclaimer for those who are prone to get offended by facts, trigger warning. Facts don't care about your feelings. With that formally out of the way, let's begin.

I'll start with the most personal of these ideas, the idea that systemic racism is still alive and well. This idea is held up using evidence like the disproportionate number of blacks in prison, disproportionate amounts of traffic stops, stop and frisks, lack of great education, and other issues plaguing the black community. If you think I haven't been that informative enough for you so far, hold onto your seat. Where to begin, where to begin. Ok, like before I will give you the facts, feel free to fact check me, in fact, PLEASE do. Fact #1, despite making up just 13.3 percent of the population we are responsible for 52.4 percent of murders and 54.9 percent of robberies. Compare that to whites who make up 76.9 percent of the population and are responsible for 45.2 percent of murders and 43.4 percent of robberies, and these are just 2 of the many crimes that are committed in this country. If you were to go down the list of the FBI crime statistics, you would find a troubling truth, blacks in almost every category commit a disproportionate amount of crime with respect to their population. It is important to point out that it is not the fact that blacks are black that this occurs, but it is because of the culture that blacks adopt that we see these disparities. Mainstream "Black Music" has been known to, more often than not, encourage violence, drug use, and glorified those who are "Thugs" ready to pop a cap in someone's a**. Some black youth in poverty, who are more focused on their education than the others, are called house niggers among other things. These have an adverse effect on black youth making it out of where they are, causing some to change for the worse. These are just a few of many. Fact #2, single motherhood is out of control in the black community, not exclusively though(clarification for those prepared to accuse me of implying it is just the black community). From 2011 to 2015, single-parent families were around 67 percent in the black community. Compare that to the non-Hispanic whites which were steady around 25 percent. It is again not about being black; it is about the culture that a large portion of blacks adopts. Mainstream "Black Music" has been known to, more often than not, encourage people to "smash," aka have sex with, as many babes as you can.

You can't be ridiculed for thinking that a group of black male youth hanging out are probably talking about the multitude of ladies they are trying to get into. It is obviously not just black youth, by no stretch. But what most of these groups have in common, regardless of race, is probably the music they listen to and the artist they idolize. When accompanied by the fact that for whatever reason fathers aren't staying with the women they impregnate, the data isn't surprising. Fact #3, being fatherless is a strong indicator of whether you will be more likely to follow a life of crime or not. Studies have shown, although what I could find are a bit dated, 71 percent of all high school dropouts come from fatherless homes, 75 percent of all adolescents in chemical abuse centers are fatherless, and 85 percent of adolescence in prison are from fatherless homes. All these facts put into consideration, and you see that it is not systemic racism that is holding most of us blacks back, it is a culture that makes it difficult to succeed by encouraging some not so positive actions. Worst of all, blaming all your problems on whites and this false premise of systematic racism is blinding us to the actual problems, and this is going to make it even more difficult to come together and resolve them. I know if you are on the left, you will probably call me a coon or a brainwashed black boy, but the facts don't lie. We should encourage black youth to refrain from having sex with multiple partners not preparing for the possibility of raising their kid. We should encourage them to hit the books not hit others, and put down the guns and pick up the Bible they were raised on. We should tell them that it is up to them individually to make the right choices to make them successful and that there is no imaginary outside force holding them back. I wasn't a perfect kid, I was exposed to some of this, but I took responsibility for my actions and my life, and kept myself from going in the deep end. Anyone who tells you you can't succeed because you are black doesn't know a damn thing. Do not listen to those who say you can't, whoever they may be.

Now that we have talked about systemic racism, it's logical to follow up by talking about the myth of systemic sexism. So, the left has been propagating the stat that women on are learning 77 cents on the dollar to men, then using this to state that this is the fault of the patriarchy holding them back. Let me straighten up this BS, so all the women who have kept reading this book can know there is no outside force keeping them from achieving their full potential. I'm sure you're used to how I come at these by now, so I'll just get to it. Fact #1, if you factor in the fields that women chose to follow, the hours they usually work, amount of time off they take(generally for family issues like giving birth and raising kids), the overtime they take advantage of, and the amount of times they ask for raises the wage gap is virtually eliminated. Fact #2, wages and earnings are different things, the wage gap is actually an earnings gap. With all factors from the previous fact put into an account and the fact that men are more likely to go to more high-income fields(ex. STEM and engineering), usually take advantage of overtime more, are more willing to ask for a raise, and don't take a lot of time off. It makes sense that there is an EARNINGS gap.

Fact #3, it is illegal to pay someone less for the same work based on their sex. So, if women are indeed being paid less than men simply for being born with 2 X chromosomes, we should be drowning in lawsuits and workplace discrimination… but we're not. Fact #4, in 147 of the 150 biggest cities in the US, women earn more than man(about 8% more). To close this BS, women, you can do whatever you set your mind to and the only person out there who cares enough to get in your way is you.

Ok now, let's relax a bit and move on to the dumbest, unintellectual, and insane thing the left is now preaching about. For those who don't pay attention to the news and social issues, hold on to something. So apparently, a person who is born a biological male can become a woman, and female becomes a man. You're probably wondering why I used female and women, as well as, male and man. I did so to point out that they are interchangeable, because they are the same thing. XX= female, woman and XY=male, man. Science is very very clear on this, but today in our advanced society if a man feels like he is a woman, we must abandon all reality and call him a women. Those who believed they were the opposite gender at one point in time were considered mentally ill. It was classified as gender-dysphoria. Now, you must treat them as if they are what they say they are, and if you don't, you will be chastised and called all kinds of names for believing that science and reason is more important than social constructs. This is not even the worst of it, from this abandoning of reality, more nonsense has come to power. Now one can be one gender one day and another gender the next. In fact there are more than two genders, last I checked the number of genders has shot up to somewhere in the 60s. This is a big reason I voted for Trump as well. I'm someone who strives to gain knowledge and loves facts, and the other side is blatantly ignoring facts just to appeal to a few mentally ill people definitely going to make my choice simpler.

Alright, I have talked about some of the semi-ridiculous positions that put me off when it came to even kinda wanting to vote Democrat. I saved the most ridiculous and worrying for last. The left doesn't believe in the most important value this country was built on. That important value is so significant, an it is number one in our bill of rights, yeah that's right; they have a problem with free speech. They believe that some speech should not fall under the category of free speech. You wouldn't believe who would get to decide what should be allowed or not, guess. If you can't figure it out, I'll tell you. And if you say a man is a man and a woman is a woman that is considered hate speech and isn't covered over free speech. If you say illegal immigration is a problem, and we should deport those who commit crimes and are here illegally, then you are partaking in hate speech, and you aren't covered under free speech. Once free speech is undermined and the left appoint people, who believe in the same things that they do, to say what is fair game to say or not, opposing opinions would be censored, and the population would only hear one side of every argument and we would fall into a chaotic world run by leftists and snowflakes. You are probably thinking Mr, Author that would never happen.

I would simply point to the overwhelming majority of colleges in the US today and say no more. When the election was going on, riots would erupt when a conservative speaker dared to come speak at a college campus, MILO at the University of Berkeley is probably the best example of this. And if you think it was just some bad students and outside protesters who were trying to stop free speech you are sadly mistaken, university professors and administrators actively went out of their way to get in the way of or stop the college Republicans who wanted to host these events. They would price them up the wazoo or change the agreements and shifting deadlines to keep events from happening. The fight for free speech is under attack, and it is the left that is trying to unhinge what is pivotal in making our country the greatest country God has ever allowed to come into existence. This is where kids are being taught how they should think and how to become adults. If the left thinks this is the way to go when it comes to free speech, I am very, very, very happy I voted against their poster woman for the future of our country.

5

POLICIES

I bet you weren't expecting all these facts and in depth topics when you picked up this book. You are probably psyched about that, or you are just reading on because you paid for it, and you think what the heck I might as well get my money's worth. Either way, I hope you are at the very least learning a thing or too, or maybe you are even thinking of revisiting a stance you were previously completely sure in. I meant it when I said I was going to explain why I voted for Trump. Now, that I have covered the black history and deconstructed the unintelligent positions on the other side, I want to talk about the more serious issues that helped me make them out of the ordinary political choice I made. For a heads up, these are issues like taxes, healthcare, big government, education, immigration, and welfare; these won't be their own stories, but just a quick glimpse of what I think and some facts to help support why I voted Republican, I promise.

The first of these big issues are taxes, this is a big topic for every American regardless of race, sex, or economic class. These dreaded taxes come in a few forms, like state taxes that are different for everyone depending on your state of residence or federal taxes that everyone feels regardless of where you're at in the states. The main aspects of taxes are how they are obtained, and what they are used for. And for simplicity's sake, I will just talk about those. The most important of these to is what they are used for. Taxes are used for defense, security, healthcare, welfare, social security, among many others. Ultimately, it is our defense that should be getting the bulk of our taxes; it should go to the troops and our military to protect us from any outside force that could destroy our great country. Outside of that and things like police, firefighters, and other agencies that keep peace and protect us in everyday life, I think our taxes should be used very little for anything else. It is not and should not be the government's job to take care of your medical expenses, bad financial decisions, and bad life decisions. If you did not save and invest your money throughout your life it should not be the government's job to take care of you. If you decided to have kids before marriage, dropout of school, or not try to find a job, it shouldn't be the government's job to take care of you and/or your kids. The government is funneling our hard earned money to people who did not and do not make a good life and financial decisions, and it is those who are doing the right things with their lives and money who are FORCED to pay for them. This is where many people have a problem with taxes and rightly so. And the biggest thing, as a Christian and just a caring human being, what angers me about our taxes is that some of it goes towards organizations like Planned Parenthood who murder and make money from unborn babies. Regardless of where you line up on the Pro-life or Pro-choice issue I, a taxpayer, should not be forced to pay for the murder of babies. Taxes were made for protections and things that are necessary for citizens; little more should even be considered. Citizens should take care of their business without my money being taken from me to pay for their mistakes. That's that. As you can tell where my taxes go means a lot to me, who has less in the pocket because of it.

Where taxes go is a bigger deal than where they come from, because it is the necessities that cause us to have to pay taxes in the first place. Now that I have explained and expressed issues surrounding where our taxes go let's talk about how we get the money in the first place, and this is what gets the most spotlight. We the citizens are forced to pay taxes, and we are willing to because it is supposed to provide us with protection and necessities that the private sector shouldn't be competing for.

The issues arise when we talk about how much of our money the government should be taking for these taxes and from whom they take them. The big talk in the media and the left is the talk of the top percentile of earners in the country paying more of their fair share in taxes. The problem with this is apparently, fair share means if you make more, the government should take more of your hard earned money. I've always wondered why we don't just pay a flat tax; you pay a percentage of how much you make and everyone pays that same percentage. But that's not the way we have it in this country, those who make, more have to pay a higher percentage of what they make simply because they have made the right decisions that brought them more income. And those on the left lean a tad bit too far on the socialist side and think the rich should have more taken from them just so those at the bottom can be given money to catch up to the rest. This infuriates me, you can take more of my money simply because I have more, if you look at it deeper, it's stealing from the rich, and I don't know about you, but stealing is against my religion and should be frowned upon, regardless of what you're stealing for. It is alright though, since the rich can learn and hire people who can help them keep the government from taking more of their money, while operating within the limits of the law. But wait, how dare they, they shouldn't be allowed to do that. What makes them think they shouldn't be paying more than everyone else simply because they are more successful? Those greedy capitalists try and keep more of the money they worked hard for to themselves!! Taxes are a more miniscule issue that helped me vote Republican, this is only because I wasn't making that bank at the time, but I plan on it, and I do not want a larger percentage of my money taken from me simply because I worked harder.

This sickens me, even more, when it's clear that too much of that money is going to those who didn't make good financial and life decisions, and is being taken from me and funneled into their pockets!!

A BIG issue is health care. Before I continue, this must be clarified; healthcare is not a right, it is a commodity. You don't have the right to make a nurse who devoted a good amount of her life to nursing school to take care of you. That would be in the simplest words slavery. Regardless of if your socialist overlord Bernie Sanders has told you, you don't have a right to someone's services. Anyways, now that I have got that out of the way, single-payer healthcare is horrible and everywhere it is implemented quality drops and wait times increase at ridiculous rates. Oh, before I lose your attention, Obama Care is trash and should never have been passed. Ask all those who were promised better prices, but instead got higher prices (30% increases per year for many), fewer options, having to pay for things they don't need, oh and worst of all now they are punished if you don't have insurance, so they are essentially forcing you to buy anyways. This was a big reason I voted for Trump; he said he would get rid of this discussing filth forced upon us by a horrible president, who made it law by overstepping his power. It is clear that when the government gets involved in the private sector, things don't work out well for all of us. If the government stops subsidizing, heavily regulating, and dictating what happens in the healthcare market, companies will be able to compete for their customers. This translates to better prices and better quality for consumers, but you won't hear about this truth much, because the left loves big government even if it is bad for the American people.

Next on the serious issues is education, and boy, do I have a bone to pick with our modern education system. First off, I hate the fact that the left dominates education, twisting history to help their political ideology, especially in college. Although I'd love to use this time to rip them a new one, I am talking about the bigger situations, like school choice and how to better the education of those who are essentially the future of our great country. The biggest concern with the education at this time is the lack of quality that is given to students in various parts of the country, especially the urban areas. The problem is somewhat complicated, bad teachers aren't being fired, and parents don't have the option to send kids to better schools due to lack of school choice. The solution is found in the free market system that our country thrives on. Allow parents to choose what schools, and have the funding follow the children This would cause schools to compete for your child to attend their schools. This would drastically improve the quality of the education that the students would receive. When parents can decide what education is good enough for their kids, it becomes the schools that have to compete and raise their quality to reach the levels that the parents want. I know this sounds like such an easy solution that everyone should be on board with, but sadly, that is not the case. People on the other side don't want this to happen for whatever reason, and it is at the expense of the youth that deserve a shot at the best. Another factor of education that shouldn't be looked over is the rise of charter schools. This goes hand in hand with giving parents the choice. The more and better choices, the better the quality has to be to get your child. Charter schools have been shown to be very effective in producing stellar results for students, and that's exactly what every parent is looking for when it comes to the education for the most precious people in their lives. There are many more aspects of education, but these are the most pivotal and having these resolved would cause the others to fall in line. Oh, and just in case you didn't get the message at the beginning of this issue, keep the left's political agenda out of our kids' education!!!.

The last of the more serious issues that led me to vote for Trump is the state of our welfare state. This goes hand in hand with immigration. Welfare in it of itself is a semi-socialist institution; it essentially takes money from those who have and helps send it to those who have not. I understand that this is for a "good" reason, but it always spirals out of control. When you start to give people things for seemingly nothing in return, they begin to ask for more and more and more. Before you know it, you are stuck. They become more and more dependent, on you and you put yourself in a position that you become responsible for them. This is precisely what has become of our welfare system. People are cheating the system, some even making a good income living entirely off the government. And if the government were to take this from them there would be riots in the streets, and there would be significant ramifications on our economy. Though some believe that it has already ventured beyond the point of no return, I say we are America, and we can overcome anything. Welfare should become more strict on what qualifies you for assistance and how long you are allowed to receive this assistance. It is known that people have been allowed to keep receiving welfare checks long after when they're limit is up. It is known that people will have kid, after kid, after kid, to get more from the government. There are more abuses of this welfare and if we want our country to survive, we need to get rid of it and encourage people to take responsibility for their own lives and financial situations instead of relying on the Government to continue being their parents. On a separate but related issue, illegal immigration is out of control, and with the current state of our welfare system, they are collecting welfare checks as well. This DRIVES ME INSANE. My hard earned tax dollars are going to people who don't work, exploit the system, or aren't supposed to be in the country in the first place. Welfare and immigration are a big deal, and Trump was very vocal about trying to stop these catastrophic problems, while the other side wanted to be complacent or increase the problem. This is one of, if not Trump's most important promises and it's about time we had someone in the white house who would do something to truly bring an end to this.

5

THE AFTERMATH

Now that I have gone through all reasons why I voted for Trump, it's time to give a brief rundown of what's happened after the election. As you all know, my boy President Trump won, much to the despair of all those on the left. Since that historic underdog victory, the country has gone a bit crazy. People immediately tried to delegitimize the election, the very same people who told Trump he should accept the results. Hoards of kids, rioting and chanting, "Not my president," through the streets. Media and the Hollywood elite challenging the electoral college to go against their voters and not vote Trump in. The Trump and Russia conspiracy being covered as if it were a fact. Borderline terrorism was raging on during the inauguration. Irreverent singers were chanting about how they have thought an awful lot about blowing up the white house. This was just a few things that preceded the election, but it's all good though because the more people act like children on the other side, the more they are giving campaign contributions to Trump's reelection in 2020.

Some great things have happened since the election as well. The rise of Antifa has finally got the somewhat truthful coverage it deserved, and now, those who previously were complacent in their actions (cough cough CNN and other leftist media outlets) even going so far as defending them, are forced to report that they are a violent group. As of this moment, Antifa is finally classified as a domestic terrorist organization. Pretty soon, BLM will follow. Trump is trying to push for some serious tax reform. Louder with Crowder is taking the world by storm and even infiltrating terrorist groups, doing real investigative work(CNN take notes). Ben Shapiro is going in the belly of the leftist beast and is causing devastation in a magnitude that is shaking up the country and needing 600k to keep him safe to do so. Disrespectful head smashers at the NFL are disrespecting our anthem and by extension our country and our president is speaking out against it, and the American people are standing against it. There are others, but these are some of the biggest ones that have caught my eye.

6

CONCLUSION

If you have made it all the way to this point, I truly do appreciate it. If you are on the same side as me, I hope you at least learned a little more in this book. If you don't agree, I hope you at least got to see into the mind of someone on the other side. Also, I respect the fact that you read it all the way through. If you are not politically inclined and just picked up this book because it was well priced and seemed somewhat interesting, I hope you leave with a little more interest in at least some of the topics I've touched. Sorry, I don't have some brilliant conclusion to leave you with, but I've got one that has come to convey the right message to those of all races, sexes, religions, creeds, backgrounds, political ideologies, and other aspects of every individual; God bless you, and God bless America!!

About The Author

I am Nicaleb Gedeon, I am an American of Haitian descent, for those that don't know, that means I was born in the United States and my parents are both immigrants from Haiti. I was born in Boca Raton, FL, and moved to Green Cove Springs, FL when I was in third grade. I have never written a book before which you might have noticed, but I'll get the hang of it. I was raised Seventh Day Adventist, but in my senior year of highschool I asked a question to a religious teacher of mine, and the answer he gave me sent me on a path of serious research. That research caused me to realise that they weren't biblically accurate in some of their core teaching, so I left that religion and now I am non-denominational, but gravitate more to the Baptist beliefs. I love music, knowledge, and debating. I am what some would call a nerd, I love anime(mostly Dragon Ball Z), Game of Thrones, DC and Marvel movies, spending time watching videos on anything from the newest phones to documentaries on space and science. The most important thing about me is probably that I absolutely love politics, religion, and philosophy. I can talk about these topics all day, preferably with someone who doesn't agree with me, because that really challenges my thoughts and premises. So if you liked this book, there will be a lot more in store on things that fall into that category.

53828881R00036

Made in the USA
Columbia, SC
21 March 2019